Ingrid Matson Wekerle

from the Artist, for
Colleagues of the Arts Salon
at Pat + Robert Warn...
at Pebble Beach, Sept 30th,

Van Megert has a marvelous way of drawing you into his paintings.
You are there, enjoying the setting. You can almost hear the waves breaking.
This book is an exciting display of Van's work in an area he loves.
He invites you to love Pebble Beach along with him.

George P. Shultz
Former U.S. Secretary of State

S. F. B. Morse, founder of Pebble Beach
(portrait by Van Megert)

VAN MEGERT

Pebble Beachscapes™

A Coast Publishing Book

Limited Editions Press

ISBN 1-930210-00-0

Limited Editions Press
Post Office Box 11855
Lahaina, Maui, Hawaii 96761

For further information on art by Van Megert
please contact Coast Gallery Pebble Beach
Pebble Beach, California 93953
(831) 624-2002 • www.coastgalleries.com

List of Paintings

1. S. F. B. Morse
2. Courtyard Garden
3. Dunes at Spyglass Hill
4. Cypress and Deer
5. Treasures at Pebble Beach
6. Covey of Quail
7. Beach Rocks at Pebble Beach
8. 7th at Pebble Beach
9. Spanish Bay Dunes
10. Raccoons
11. Storm off Pebble Beach
12. Bing Crosby
13. 18th at Pebble Beach
14. The Castle
15. South Coast from Pebble Beach
16. Lodge from 18th Tee
17. Pines at Pebble Beach
18. Drifting Fog, Stillwater Cove
19. Deer Family
20. White Sand at Pebble Beach
21. Cypress Grove
22. Daisies at Pebble Beach
23. Lone Cypress

Vistas and Visions

Pebble Beachscapes is about an artist and an area, about vision and preservation, about being gifted and sharing the gift. It is about the ability of one man to see into the future, and about another's portrayal of the results. This is a book about scenic grandeur protected by one man and painted by another; it reveals the enduring beauty of one of the most precious areas known to man—Pebble Beach, California.

Two visionaries, an entrepreneur and an artist, made this book possible.

S. F. B. Morse, a land developer and California conservationist, founded Pebble Beach. His life's work resulted in the preservation of the area's shoreline and forest, its wilderness and animal life. As man is not apart from his environs, Morse developed a master plan whereby people could live in the very place being protected—a plan designed to achieve harmony between man and nature. Pebble Beach is enjoyed daily by its residents and visitors, while at the same time being preserved for future generations. It is perhaps the closest vision of paradise on earth that a mere man could achieve.

Van Megert, an artist who migrated from Oregon to California and settled in Pebble Beach, has spent over fifty years with a brush in hand, searching for and finding beauty to paint. Born an artist, having created his first portrait at six, he has painted Pebble Beach hundreds of times during his thirty years of residence. Van Megert's lifelong dream has been to create images of beauty infused with peace and tranquillity. Who better to memorialize S. F. B. Morse's legacy? Van Megert paints one of the world's loveliest places, one the artist calls "God's home," and he does so with grace and humility.

Pebble Beachscapes reveals the artist's versatility. He captures all aspects of this remarkable area, a great diversity of natural elements. There is a purity of presence in these environs that inspires Van Megert to paint their every nook and cranny, their many moods and mysteries.

When asked what he most likes to paint, the artist responds with childlike innocence, thrilled by everything in sight and anxious to record it all—not fearing it will disappear, but eager to paint it while he can. With no favorite motif, he paints people and animals, forest and rocks, land and sea—all the scapes of Pebble Beach.

Van Megert paints golfdom's most beautiful kingdom, with its subtle mystique and magnificence. With a rainbow palette, he captures Pebble's beachscapes in their many moods, from hazy mists and lapping surf to foggy forests and crimson sunsets. He paints wildflowers, florals and gardens with the same ease as he renders glorious mansions and sprawling estates. No beauty made by God or man escapes his eye or eludes his canvas. Everything in Pebble Beach is a painting. Even his abstract works are micro visions writ large of rock formations on a pebbled beach or gnarled branches in a cypress grove. And as a portrait artist, Van Megert has painted Pebble's people—from the founder himself, Sam Morse, to Bing Crosby, Bob Hope, Gerald Ford and George Shultz, among many others.

Van Megert speaks rarely to others of the Creator, the acknowledged source of his talent, although he surely speaks to Him more often than not. How else could he see, let alone paint, nature's glory in a way that evokes such peace of mind?

Ah, to leave behind what Morse and Megert have left! Such legacies will not be forgotten. To visit Morse's Pebble Beach, much less live there, is a blessing unto itself. Van Megert's paintings are nature preserved, transformed into art, and lastingly available to all. Both men have given us vistas and visions of that very special place we call Pebble Beach.

Gary Koeppel
Founder, Coast Galleries and Publishing

Detail from Courtyard Garden
Original 18 inches by 24 inches

Painting 2

I came to Pebble Beach when I knew I had to do something with my career. I had to leave Oregon, because in 1968 there just wasn't a way to make a living there as an artist. I decided to visit all the art communities in California—Mendocino, Laguna, La Jolla and Carmel. I ended up in Carmel, an art colony next to Pebble Beach. I joined the Carmel Art Association and started to sell my work immediately. I visited Pebble Beach often, fell in love with it, and was able to find a place in the Del Monte Forest. I've been here ever since—for thirty years.

Pebble Beach is simply beautiful. It has a little bit of everything—mountains and trees, ocean and animals, and superb golf. Everywhere you look is a painting. It's very inspiring, and I've noticed the difference. When I go back to Oregon on a visit, I don't have the inspiration I find in Pebble. Oregon is also beautiful, but you have to travel long distances to see all its areas. Pebble Beach is—what's the word—encapsulated? It has everything right at your fingertips—mountains and the ocean at the same time. The Monterey Peninsula is a natural home for artists because it is a perfect place for them to work and grow. It's also a small town with a lot of quietude and privacy, which I find necessary in my work. I enjoy traveling and painting in Europe, but if I never took another trip, I think I'd have all I want right here in Pebble Beach.

Courtyard Garden

Detail from Dunes at Spyglass Hill
Original 16 inches by 22 inches

Painting 3

I was born in Salem, Oregon in 1938 and went to schools there. The northwest is a beautiful area with dramatic seasonal changes—at first I had a hard time adjusting to Pebble Beach because this area is subtler. It took a while to acclimate to gentle seasonal changes.

People ask if I had any artists in my family. I believe some were artistically talented but were too busy raising families to pursue an artistic career.

I've wanted to paint since I was six years old. I really don't know where it came from. I wanted to paint portraits, which is unusual, I'm told. And I've always had confidence from knowing what I was going to do. My friends didn't decide what they wanted until they were in college—and some even after graduation. They had an insecurity that I never knew, but there's a down side. When you're sure about your work, you don't even try to do other things. All I know how to do is paint.

Dunes at Spyglass Hill

Detail from Cypress and Deer
Original 48 inches by 48 inches

Painting 4

Once I began, I started painting everything. I copied old masters when I was seven. When you're going to school, you don't have much chance to paint. Sometimes I wouldn't paint anything for six months, and when I started again there had been growth even though I hadn't been painting. As I matured it was reflected in my creative work. I know a lot of people who have painted all their lives, but they've never grown as artists because they refused to look at things. I believe if you observe the world without concentrating so much on actual painting, you're still developing in how you see. During my school days, painting was limited to spurts of time. I might set it aside and not finish for weeks, but I was always working on something.

Cypress and Deer

Detail from Treasures at Pebble Beach
Original 48 inches by 48 inches

Painting 5

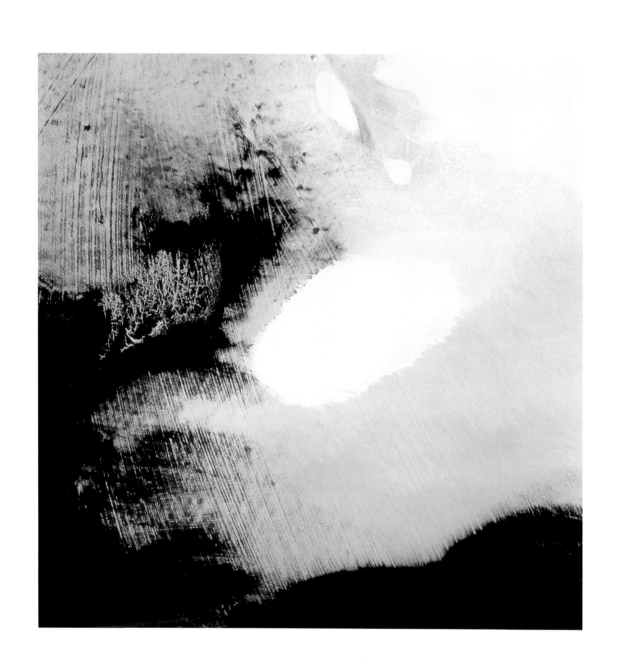

You must have a reason to begin a painting, not just say "I'm going to get up and paint." You need the incentive of whether you want to do a portrait, a landscape or an abstract. At least that's the way I paint. Many abstract painters don't know what's happening, where it's going or how it will work out. I think the beginning is knowing where you want to go, and then let it paint itself.

I believe everybody wants to create something, although they might not be artistically or musically inclined. Anyone can be artistic, whether a housewife, a teacher—anyone who is creating something, not necessarily a painting. A famous conductor, when asked his secret of success, replied "Whatever I do, I put my whole heart into it, whether I'm conducting an orchestra or peeling an orange."

Treasures at Pebble Beach

Detail from Covey of Quail
Original 14 inches by 22 inches

Painting 6

People have asked how I learned painting. First you have to learn how to draw. That's the hardest part, but I think anybody can learn to draw. It takes time and patience; you can take classes or not; it's just a technical thing that you need to do. When you're actually painting you shouldn't have to think about how to draw. You should be thinking of more intrinsic things. When I studied the piano, it was impossible to learn which keys to play because you're playing so fast. Your fingers memorize the keys. There isn't time to think about each note, your fingers must know the notes. In painting you don't think about drawing, you just do it while painting.

When I received an art scholarship to Willamette University I was finally able to paint intensely for a period of two years. I was fortunate to study with the artist in residence, Carl Hall, who was very prominent in the area. As a child I went to his one-man shows and admired him and his work. It was my dream to study with him. I took all of his classes and learned a lot; it took two years. Then I got bored, walked off the campus one day, and never went back.

Covey of Quail

Detail from Beach Rocks at Pebble Beach
Original 36 inches by 60 inches

Painting 7

Detail from 7th at Pebble Beach
Original 20 inches by 24 inches

Painting 8

My folks had purchased a place in the country with several buildings. After leaving college, I had my own cabin. I turned it into a studio—lived and worked there, and just painted for the next 5 or 6 years. I'd been working and had saved enough money to live frugally. I got my first two or three hundred paintings out of the way—threw most of them away, stuck my foot through many, but at least I learned my craft.

I began painting with oils, but they take forever because you have to wait for each layer to dry. I like to paint fast and in layers. When I learned about acrylics and how fast they set up, I could do a painting in a few days that would have taken a month with oils. I also learned that acrylic is similar to an egg tempera medium. Egg temperas painted on board in the 15th and 16th centuries are still beautiful, whereas later Flemish and other artists turned to oil, painting on linen or parchment. The oils have deteriorated badly. Acrylics don't fade and are a very durable paint medium.

7th at Pebble Beach

Detail from Spanish Bay Dunes
Original 48 inches by 48 inches

Painting 9

I like the feeling of painting on board rather than canvas. With linen you must deal with stretcher bars; when shipping a painting on board, it's more durable and doesn't get damaged. For some reason, you can always improve a painting by cutting it down. I invariably end up cropping a painting, which is easier if painted on board. However, the largest sheet of Masonite measures 4 x 8 feet, and some of my paintings are larger. For big commissions I do paint on canvas, and I enjoy that too.

The hardest part is deciding what you want to paint. You have to get an idea and see it in your mind, and almost know what you want it to look like when you're finished. Usually the painting is much different from originally imagined, but at least you got started. Things always happen you hadn't planned on, and that's what makes the act of painting spontaneous and creative. I call them happy accidents.

Spanish Bay Dunes

Detail from Raccoons
Original 16 inches by 22 inches

Painting 10

I don't know whether creativity is the motivator or the end result of a painting. It could be either way. Everybody's different, and everybody's approach is different. Thank God that artists differ, with various reasons for doing what they do. For some it could be vanity, perhaps others want to be somebody. In the end, who they are shows up in the work. If they are shallow and painting for glamour, their careers won't last long. They'll get pretty bored with it.

Some of my best days are when I've gotten up and painted something I was very proud of, whether or not it ever sold. It didn't matter, the work made me happy. Doing something I feel is mediocre never gives me pleasure. However, when your paintings sell, and people spend money on work you've done, you realize maybe you do have something to offer. It's nice to be paid for a painting. It's a way of knowing that you are appreciated, and it's an incentive to paint. Painting can be a rather insecure existence; it's not a concerted effort with others who give you moral support. You're alone; you can feel very uncertain, and sometimes you think that painting is pure folly. But when you're remunerated and appreciated, you feel you can go on with it.

Raccoons

Detail from Storm off Pebble Beach
Original 24 inches by 36 inches

Painting 11

I've often been asked if painting, which is a very solitary process, is also lonely. That depends on the individual. I've never been a lonely person; in fact I fight for my time to be alone. A good artist will have friends in whom he can confide and people who will advise him. I think you should never be so proud that you can't take advice and learn from other people. Other people are part of your life, and you're painting for other people, so you should learn to listen to them, too.

I don't have a favorite subject in painting. What I'm doing at the moment is my favorite, and I'd like to be able to paint everything. I would hate to be stuck in a rut, painting the same thing over and over, as some people do. What drives me is I would like to think I'm creating art, as opposed to commercial schlock—which can happen when you do something again and again. I've repeated subjects, but I approach each painting as if I've never painted it before. Long ago an artist friend told me to always go back to the source. Don't go back to the last painting, because you're just doing that painting again. But in the original source you'll see something different. Always seeing anew is the key. Monet painted haystacks over and over, but each one was different.

Storm off Pebble Beach

Detail from Bing Crosby
Original 36 inches diameter

Painting 12

My first painting was a portrait I did when I was six years old. Probably it was just somebody I saw in a magazine. For your first paintings you do nothing but copy. I recall it was a woman wearing a green hat. I think my parents still have it someplace.

Places like Pebble Beach attract famous and interesting people. In order to succeed as an artist when you haven't established a reputation, you have to be where people go to buy paintings—areas such as Pebble Beach and Carmel. Slowly word got out that I was a portrait painter. My first portrait of a famous person was President Ford. He often visited friends in Pebble Beach, and I was commissioned to paint his portrait. I presented it to the Fords one evening, which was quite an honor. I've painted many corporate executives, their wives, families, grandchildren and pets. I was commissioned to paint a portrait of the founder of Pebble Beach, S. F. B. Morse (reproduced as the frontispiece in this book). Some celebrities I've painted include Bing Crosby, Bob Hope and Doris Day. Miss Day, an animal lover, commissioned me to paint a Pebble Beach deer family.

Bing Crosby

Detail from 18th at Pebble Beach
Original 30 inches by 36 inches

Painting 13

The hardest thing to do is face a blank canvas, because you know it's going to be a lot of intense work. There's a chance it will flop and all be a waste of time. But you have to overcome that fear—even if it is a flop, you've learned from it.

I used to play recorded classical music all the time while I painted. I studied piano for 12 years and love music, but now I find it gets in the way. I feel best in a quiet atmosphere, alone with my thoughts, concentrating only on the painting. I live in a protected bay right on the ocean; it can be very quiet at times, but exciting when the sea is active. When I leave the area on a trip, the first thing I miss is the smell and feeling of being at sea level. I don't know if those senses inspire my work, but the sound of the ocean helps me to rest. It's just wonderful to be here.

18th at Pebble Beach

Detail from The Castle
Original 16 inches by 22 inches

Painting 14

As a child I was drawn to Rembrandt because I loved his portraits, and the similar work of Frans Hals. I studied them—that's really how I taught myself to paint. Although I didn't have exposure to actual Rembrandts, there are excellent books available with fine reproductions. Sometimes you can see a painting better in a book than on the wall in a museum. The photograph is clear and perfectly lit. So I don't believe you have to make the Grand Tour to Europe, although it's wonderful if you can.

The Castle

Detail from South Coast from Pebble Beach
Original 30 inches by 40 inches

Painting 15

I enjoy very good contemporary artists. I learn more from them now; you can absorb just so much from the old masters, and you see the same work over and over. It's exciting to walk into a gallery and discover a living artist who's doing something different, and who can inspire you to take new directions. Don't ask me to name any artists—there are so many, and some are wonderful. In fact there are some better painters than the old masters, because even more is expected of an artist now. People are familiar with the masters, but they're also familiar with images through the camera that didn't exist before. If you paint a portrait or specific subject, it has to be virtually perfect. I think first-rate art is being made today.

South Coast from Pebble Beach

Detail from Lodge from 18th Tee
Original 18 inches by 36 inches

Painting 16

Detail from Pines at Pebble Beach
Original 30 inches by 40 inches

Painting 17

When I go to museums in Europe, I often walk past the famous paintings and discover an unknown artist, one who wasn't in the right place at the right time and didn't become well known. Many such painters were well trained—one wonders why they didn't achieve fame. Usually artists become prominent because they've created a unique style or technique. It might not be beautiful; they might not be well trained; but their work is different and it catches the critics' eyes.

Picasso became famous because he did things differently, but he was well trained, as one can see from his early paintings. He had the courage to abandon the traditional and take a new path. Most people tend to stick with what they know is successful. It's frightening to jump off the cliff and take a chance that may not work. But if it does, it's exciting.

Pines at Pebble Beach

Detail from Drifting Fog, Stillwater Cove
Original 36 inches by 48 inches

Painting 18

Most of the time I begin a painting with a sketch. If it's an actual scene I want to depict, I first draw it and transfer the drawing to a board or canvas, where I start painting with thin washes. I slowly build up the washes, getting the hues, darks and lights the way I want them by using heavier paint. The drawing gets lost when painted over. This is where the ability to draw comes in, so you don't lose your first idea of what you wanted.

Then the painting begins to paint itself—I just guide it. I like to think of myself as an observer. Often I've begun a painting that doesn't seem to be going anywhere, and then, before I know it, it's done. You have to learn to watch what you're doing and not over paint. Somebody once said it takes two people to paint a picture. One is the artist, and the other is someone who hits him over the head and tells him to stop painting.

Drifting Fog, Stillwater Cove

Detail from Deer Family
Original 48 inches by 48 inches

Painting 19

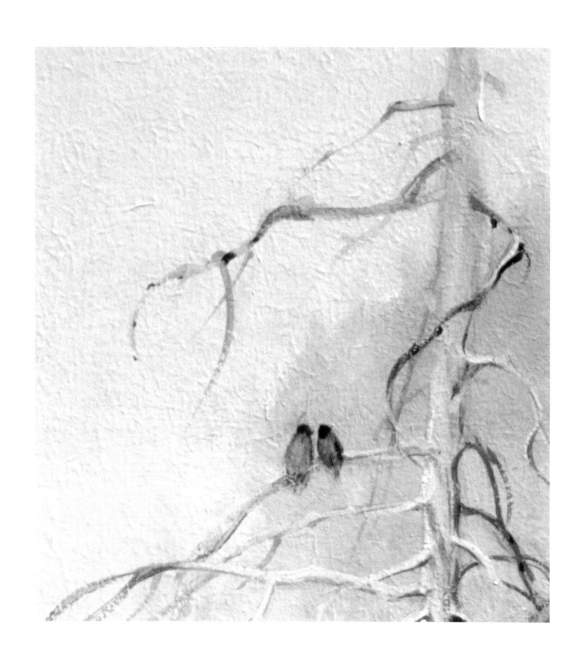

I believe that the Creator is an artist, and everything around us was created as his artistic endeavor. I think an artist is fortunate in doing something of the same thing, creating— which to me is a spiritual experience. I believe I can touch other people through my paintings. They may see something completely new, like a revelation or almost a spiritual experience.

It gets down to the artist's basic ability to look at something as if he's never seen it before, not childish but childlike. If you can retain a childlike interest in the things around you, discover something as if for the first time, then each time you paint it will be different. That's what an artist is obligated to do.

Deer Family

Detail from White Sand at Pebble Beach
Original 36 inches by 48 inches

Painting 20

I sometimes wish I had a more interesting life. I feel my paintings are more interesting than I am—I'm no competition. I'm not a personality, and I've lived a very quiet life. But I'm not complaining. That's the way I like it.

My philosophy is simple: being creative and trying to reach people through my work. Otherwise I'd feel like I was wasting my time. If you're not doing something that you consider worthwhile, you get pretty depressed. And I think that's what happens to a lot of people who have jobs they don't really enjoy. There's a lot of depression even suicides, because they're not happy with what they're doing. A creative person should realize the power to create is very rewarding, spiritually and mentally. It is a gift and one should be grateful for the gift, and shouldn't just say it's nothing—because it is something. When people used to praise me, I'd be embarrassed and say, oh, it's nothing. But now I say thank you.

White Sand at Pebble Beach

Detail from Cypress Grove
Original 24 inches by 36 inches

Painting 21

Knowing when a painting is done and done right is instinctive. I think that's really what makes an artist what he is. Of course much of it is training—you have to know certain compositions that work well on a flat plane. You have to create a certain amount of tension in the way things are arranged. Sometimes I'll work on a painting and know something's wrong with it but can't put my finger one it, so I work until it's right.

Cypress Grove

Detail from Daisies at Pebble Beach
Original 30 inches by 40 inches

Painting 22

What I hope to attain is peace; I think everybody wants that. If I have the choice of purchasing a painting to hang on my wall, I want it to be beautiful, peaceful—all the things we hope life will give us. Of course life also gives us a lot of pain and a lot of misery, but if you can offset with more positive elements, you can learn to survive. That's what I try to show in my paintings—the peaceful side. Even a stormy ocean can be beautiful—not frightening, but beautiful. I try to bring out beauty in everything I paint, even abstracts. I don't want to produce scary or depressing work. It has to be beautiful.

Daisies at Pebble Beach

Detail from Lone Cypress
Original 24 inches by 36 inches

Painting 23

I believe that an artist is remembered by his best paintings. He shouldn't worry about his mediocre works, because every artist does them. I've made hundreds of paintings, but only a few I'm really proud of. These are the ones I'd like to be remembered by— and I'd also like to be remembered as a good person.

I'm constantly growing; it's exciting to see what's around the corner. If you become jaded and don't want to paint anymore, there's something wrong. You need to sit down and analyze yourself. You might feel you've painted everything and done everything, but you can do it again and do it better.

Many artists do some of their best work when they're old, because they've grown. I want to keep growing as an artist, so I'll keep painting for the rest of my life, God willing.

Lone Cypress